CUTTING-EDGE TECHNOLOGY

ALL ABOUT
CODING

by Angie Smibert

FOCUS
READERS

WWW.NORTHSTAREDITIONS.COM

Produced for North Star Editions by Red Line Editorial.

Photographs ©: Rawpixel.com/Shutterstock Images, cover, 1, 14–15, 23; OlegDoroshin/Shutterstock Images, 4–5; Fine Art Images Heritage Images/Newscom, 7; Everett Historical/Shutterstock Images, 9; Johan Swanepoel/Shutterstock Images, 10–11; Red Line Editorial, 13; michaeljung/Shutterstock Images, 17; Scratch: Scratch is developed by the Lifelong Kindergarten Group at the MIT Media Lab. See http://scratch.mit.edu., 18–19; eakkaluktemwanich/Shutterstock Images, 20–21; Jason Ogulnik/picture-alliance/dpa/AP Images, 24–25; Tony Avelar/AP Images, 27; Shizuo Kambayashi/AP Images, 29

Content Consultant: Jeffrey Miller, Associate Professor of Engineering Practice, Department of Computer Science, University of Southern California

ISBN
978-1-63517-011-5 (hardcover)
978-1-63517-067-2 (paperback)
978-1-63517-172-3 (ebook pdf)
978-1-63517-122-8 (hosted ebook)

Library of Congress Control Number: 2016949760

Printed in the United States of America
Mankato, MN
November, 2016

ABOUT THE AUTHOR

Angie Smibert is the author of several young adult science fiction novels, including the Memento Nora series, numerous short stories, and many educational titles. She was also a writer and web developer at NASA's Kennedy Space Center for many years.

TABLE OF CONTENTS

CHAPTER 1

YOUR FIRST CODE

The bell rings, and you rush to coding club. You're excited to continue working on your video game. In the game, a queen has to find her way through a maze. On one side of your screen, you see the maze and the character you made. On the other side is a white space.

All video games have code that makes them work.

In the middle are colored blocks with commands on them. These blocks will make the queen move. You drag a block to the white space. The command on the block says WHEN RUN. You drop more blocks underneath it. They say MOVE FORWARD, TURN RIGHT, and MOVE FORWARD. When you click the run button, your hero moves forward, turns right, and moves forward again. Your code is working!

Visual coding languages are easy and fun ways to learn coding. A code, or program, is simply a set of instructions telling the computer what to do. Coding is the act of writing those instructions.

Early computers were so big that they took up entire rooms.

Coding has been around longer than computers themselves. Ada Lovelace wrote the first code in 1843 for a computer that existed only on paper. She showed how the computer could be programmed to do complex calculations.

The first computers were not built until the 1930s. A computer called Colossus was designed during World War II (1939–1945). But Colossus did not have a written code to tell it what to do. Instead, its programmers had to set the computer's plugs and switches in a new position every time the computer ran.

Programmers soon realized they needed an easier way to give computers instructions. One of the first programming languages, FORTRAN, was invented in the 1950s. Other languages soon followed.

Since then, both computers and code have evolved. Now computers are

Alan Turing was a coding pioneer whose work contributed to Colossus.

everywhere. They sit on our desks and laps. We carry them in our pockets. Some people even have computers in their bodies to help with health problems. All of these devices run on code.

CHAPTER 2

HOW CODING WORKS

Computers need specific instructions to do anything. A program is a set of instructions a computer follows. Coders use a variety of programming languages. These include Scratch, JavaScript, C, Ruby, and many more.

But computers don't understand programming languages without help.

A computer's native language, or machine code, is made up entirely of numbers.

The code needs to be translated into the computer's native language, called machine code. The most basic instructions are called **binary**. It is a language made up of zeroes and ones. Each digit tells a tiny switch in the computer to be off or on. To tell

TRANSLATORS

Programming languages differ in how they are translated into machine code. An interpreter translates the code line by line as the program runs. This makes it easy for coders to find errors. A compiler translates the whole program into machine code before it runs. The machine code is then stored and saved separately from the source code.

| programming language (Scratch, JavaScript, etc.) | translator (interpreter or compiler) | machine code | hardware (smartphone, computer, etc.) |

All high-level programming languages are translated into machine code.

a computer to do something, coders need to flip these switches in different combinations.

Machine code is difficult for humans to read. Plus, each computer has millions of switches. That is why most coders use high-level programming languages. These languages are written in commands that are closer to human language.

CHAPTER 3

THINKING LIKE A CODER

The hardest part about coding isn't learning a programming language. The hardest part is learning to explain ideas to a machine. Computers cannot guess what you mean. All of the steps need to be broken down into smaller chunks so the computer can follow them.

Coders think logically and try to anticipate problems that might happen.

Events drive many codes. The code tells the computer how to handle an event such as a mouse click or key press. An if-then statement tells the computer what to do if something happens. For example, when you test out your code, you might notice a small problem. Your character

LOOPS

Coders don't like to type the same command over and over again. They use **loops**. A loop is part of the code that repeats itself. For instance, if you want the character to move forward 10 times, you don't have to type the same command 10 times. You simply set up a loop, and the computer runs through the command 10 times. You can also use loops with if-then statements.

Coders can learn a lot by writing a code, testing it, and fixing what didn't work.

moves through the walls of your maze. You have not told the computer what to do if the character runs into something.

To fix this problem, you could write an if-then statement. In Scratch, the command might look like this:

```
If touching color blue, then
Move -2 steps
```

PROGRAMMING AN EVENT

Imagine you want your character to move when you click an arrow key. First, you must tell the computer how to react when an arrow key is clicked. You might start by writing it out in English:

> When the left arrow key is pressed, point the character left and move 10 steps.

In Scratch, directions are spelled out in degrees. So, zero degrees is up, 90 degrees is right, 180 degrees is down, and 270 degrees is left. In Scratch, the command might look like this:

> When left arrow key pressed
> Point in direction 270
> Move 10 steps

Scratch is a popular programming language for beginners.

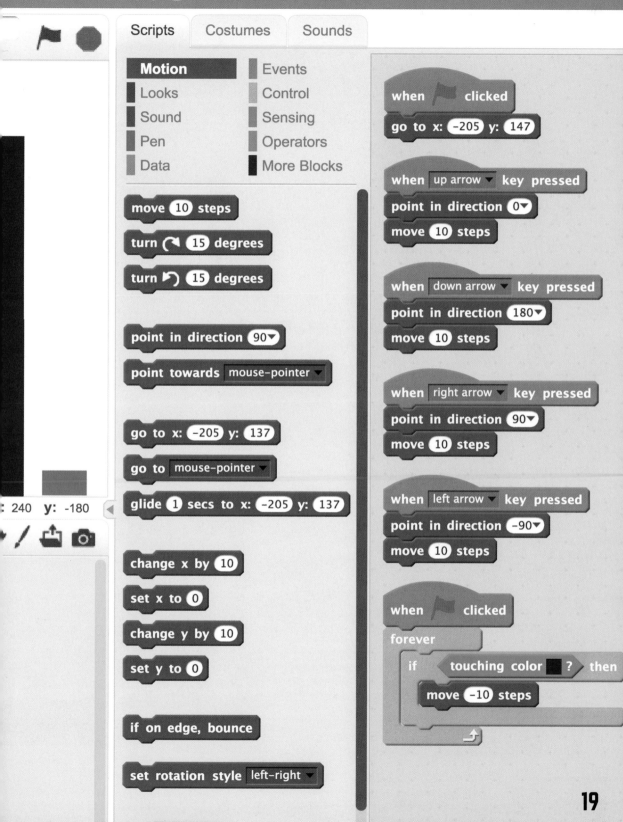

19

CHAPTER 4

AVOIDING DANGEROUS CODE

Like any tool, code can be used for destructive as well as creative purposes. Some people write code to attack computers, steal information, or spy on people. This type of code is called malware. Malware can include **viruses**, **worms**, adware, and spyware.

Malware can affect any phone, tablet, or computer if the user is not careful.

Viruses and worms are programs that can infect your device. A virus may be attached to an e-mail or downloaded from a website. When you click on the affected file, the virus's code runs. Its code might tell it to damage the device. A worm is similar to a virus. However, it does not require the user to click on the file.

Adware and spyware are programs that run in the background. Adware typically displays advertising when you're online. Spyware is a program that has been downloaded without your permission. Spyware secretly tracks your activities on your device.

Antivirus software is one way to keep a computer safe from dangerous code.

How do you protect yourself from dangerous code? First, don't click on suspicious files or links from strangers. Second, use antivirus and antimalware **software** to protect your device.

CHAPTER 5

THE FUTURE OF CODE

Today, more and more devices are connected to the Internet and to each other. It's already possible to start a car or turn on the lights at home with a smartphone. The car and the lights are connected to the Internet through code.

Thanks to code, this refrigerator can tell users when various foods are getting low.

More than five billion things are connected to the Internet. In the future, nearly every object might be connected through the Internet of Things. This is a network of devices, machines, objects, and even people. They can share data with each other without much human interaction. Each "thing" on this network would have a built-in sensor. For instance, the sensors in a car might be connected to the traffic system that monitors the roads. If an accident happens, the traffic system could tell your car to take a detour to avoid the accident.

In the past, coding has been about telling computers exactly what to do.

Google's self-driving cars use code to determine routes and to process the information that sensors gather.

These days, programmers are using code to help computers learn from experience. For instance, Netflix has computers that learn which kinds of movies you like.

They do this by keeping track of what you watch. Google's supercomputer also learned to beat human players at a board game called Go. Google coders could not write a program to tell the computer how to play Go. This task would have been too complex. The coders programmed the computer to learn. This is called machine

BIOLOGICAL COMPUTING

Another exciting area for coders is biology. In the 1990s, scientists showed how **DNA** can be used to solve certain mathematical problems. Now scientists are using DNA to store and recall data. Someday they may be able to program complex codes in living cells.

This robot, which can be used to keep elderly people company, learns the habits of its owner.

learning. The computer learned by playing the game against itself millions of times. Computers still need code, but they will use those instructions, much like humans do, to learn from experience.

FOCUS ON
CODING

Write your answers on a separate piece of paper.

1. Write a letter to a friend explaining the main ideas of Chapter 5.

2. Do you think device makers do enough to protect users from dangerous code? Why or why not?

3. What can protect your device?

   A. virus
   B. worm
   C. antimalware

4. What tells a computer what to do when the down arrow is pressed?

   A. an event
   B. a compiler
   C. a loop

Answer key on page 32.

GLOSSARY

binary

Consisting of two parts; a method for representing information by using the numbers zero and one.

DNA

The genetic material in the cells of living organisms.

events

Actions that a computer recognizes.

loops

Series of instructions that are repeated in a computer program until a specified condition is met.

software

The programs that run on a computer and perform certain functions.

viruses

Programs that are designed to harm a computer and can be spread secretly from one computer to another.

worms

Malware programs that cause damage to computers connected to each other by a network.

TO LEARN MORE

BOOKS

Briggs, Jason R. *Python for Kids*. San Francisco: No Starch, 2013.

Marji, Majed. *Learn to Program with Scratch*. San Francisco: No Starch, 2014.

McManus, Sean. *How to Code in 10 Easy Lessons*. New York: Walter Foster, 2015.

NOTE TO EDUCATORS

Visit **www.focusreaders.com** to find lesson plans, activities, links, and other resources related to this title.

INDEX

Answer Key: **1.** Answers will vary; **2.** Answers will vary; **3.** C; **4.** A